THE ORDER OF MELCHIZEDEK

D1247766

THE
ORDER
OF
MELCHIZEDEK
ALIGNING THE HIGH-PRIESTLY OFFICE
OF THE LORD JESUS WITH MELCHIZEDEK

DR. VICTOR T. NYARKO

Notion Press

Old No. 38, New No. 6
McNichols Road, Chetpet
Chennai - 600 031

First Published by Notion Press 2017
Copyright © Dr. Victor T. Nyarko 2017
All Rights Reserved.

ISBN 978-1-947349-21-6

Dedication

This book is dedicated to all the men and women of God at the Victory Family Worship Center.

Your dedication to the work of the ministry is what gives me the spare time away from some ministerial duties in order to write.

Victor T. Nyarko

OTHER EXCITING BOOKS BY

DR. VICTOR T. NYARKO

Divine Empowerment

This book is an exposition on the power of the efficacious blood of Jesus Christ, the legacy and empowerment it provided for the first Apostles, for today's believer in Jesus Christ and for all who will come after. It reveals the resources that God through Christ has made available and at our disposal for the successful accomplishment of the great commission. It also teaches the reader, how one can tap into these resources by believing it, claiming it and possessing it.

ISBN 978-1-4848-7983-2

A Disconnected Generation

This book presents striking differences between the generation of Moses and the generation of Joshua. Although Joshua's generation witnessed a glimpse of the miracles and wonder workings of God, they lacked a personal relationship with the God of their fathers and the God of Israel.

ISBN 1-59330-075-1

Dealing With Rejection

Rejection of one kind or another is inevitable throughout ones' life; therefore any tool that can be acquired to help deal with it should be a welcome choice. In this book, Dr. Nyarko presents the key elements that lead to the feeling of rejection and how to cope with rejection from a biblical perspective.

ISBN 1-59330-471-4

Beauty For Ashes

It has been the church's tradition to think that great revival could be sparked by extensive advertising, putting up the right preacher and playing the right music. If these are true ingredients for revival, then John the Baptist' revival which ignited and blazed a trail in the desolate and obscure wilderness of Judea wouldn't have had the impact it did. On the contrary, out of the ashes of repentance come revival, refreshing restitution and restoration.

ISBN 1-59330-605-9

Where Are The Fathers

The lack of fathers at home has been one of society's greatest dilemmas of our time. This book has a timely word from the Lord for everyone. God our father is calling all fathers through the pen of this godly author and father, back to the honorable and critical role of fatherhood. Get ready, Read it, Repent and pass it on.

ISBN 13: 978-1-59330-243-6

Kingdom Worship

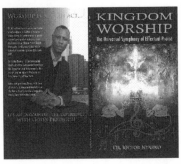

Music is part of worship but good music alone does not constitute worship. In this book, the various Hebrew words for 'praise' are described. It sheds light on the true meaning of worship and what the popular command 'Hallelujah' means in the praise and worship of God. It comes from the two Hebrew words *Halal* which is the most radical form of praise and *Yah* which is the short form for Jehovah. To worship God, goes far beyond being an act. It should be a personal encounter with God's presence which should lead to the worshipper, leaving His presence with fulfillment and gratification. In brief, this book focuses on what it means to halal (praise) God, who ought to Halal (praise) Him and where he ought to be Halal (praise).

Contents

The Order of Melchizedek

Aligning the High-Priestly Office of the Lord Jesus with Melchizedek.

Preface

This book is the fruit of a Sunday morning message that I preached on 'Melchizedek' at our church in the Bronx, New York. It was put together into a book within a week immediately following that Sunday morning service.

As I looked further into the topic after the service as I would often do after preaching a sermon, the Holy Spirit began to open the eye of my spiritual understanding so much more than I had anticipated about this strange biblical character, Melchizedek.

This book ended up being the quickest piece of work that I'd ever done so far. It was written from the Monday following the preaching of the message at church and completed by the Monday of the following week.

I was marveled by how quickly I was able to put this book together, seeing I had never done any prior studies on this topic in the past. I had the impression of having it dictated to me by some inward voice rather than writing it out myself.

As you read through the pages of the book, it's my prayer that the Lord will grant you deep revelation and greater understanding to this interesting biblical personage whose name, life, and office became a typology followed by the high priestly order of our Lord Jesus Christ.

Acknowledgements

Thank you

To

My daughter Victoria Nyarko for a superb photography.

Janet Smith, and Andrea Williams my editorial staff.

Joan Elaine my wife, life partner and my greatest counselor.

Joan Forbes my Executive Assistant,

Tori, Joash and Vanya my greatest admirers.

Chapter 1

Introduction

Melchizedek is generally recognized as the most mysterious and unaccountable of all historical bible characters. On the surface it seems as if the bible doesn't say much about Melchizedek but when I began to look closely into his name, his person and his office, I realized to my amazement and uttermost surprise that the bible says far more about him than I had ever thought.

He is mentioned nowhere else in the bible with regards to his being and person, except in the fourteenth chapter of the book of Genesis (Gen. 14:18) where he appears on the scene momentarily with Abraham and then immediately disappear.

Melchizedek disappeared from the pages of history just as suddenly as he appeared. Nothing is recorded of his family or lineage, or of his life or actions. No record was kept of his installation in his high Priestly office, his official acts, or his death, hence as far as the record is concerned, he was without beginning of days or end of life. [Condensed Biblical Cyclopedia].

He stands unique and isolated both in his person, character and in his history. His life has no recorded beginning or end, therefore he is typical of all that is mysterious and abrupt in appearance and disappearance. [Westcott, Ep. Hebrews, p. 172].

As opposed to any other bible personage, Melchizedek enters into the scene of bible history like a streak of light, for which neither the coming nor the going could easily be discerned; he's without father, without mother, without descent, having neither beginning of days, nor end of life according to the book of Hebrews. [PCH; Pulpit Commentary Homiletics]

From an excerpt from the sacred history by the great King David, in Psalm 110:4, and by the great Apostle Paul, in Hebrews 7:1-10, we learn that there must be something very mysterious and at the same time typical, in the name, person, office, and residence of Melchizedek.

Later on in the holy scriptures and hundreds of years after this one encounter with the Patriarch Abraham, we would come to find out from the pages of holy scriptures about this strange figure (i.e. in the books of Psalms and Hebrews) that His office foreshadowed the High priesthood of Christ, whose work never passes away, but who abides as a priest continually. Hence Melchizedek was a type of Christ. In other words, his life and person is being used by God to portray what the high-priestly order of Our Lord Jesus would be like. Since this priesthood would not follow the order of the Old Testament Levitical priesthood, it must therefore follow some order or pattern of another sort.

Throughout scriptures it is not strange for the personage and life of various individuals to be used as a typology of God or of his coming Christ. God used the personage and lives of Moses, Joshua (meaning Savior) David and many others in a similar manner. For Moses, his encounter with

God occurred at the unfortunate event of his striking of the rock instead of God's instructions for him to speak to the rock. Later on in the bible, and after many thousands of years later, the book of Hebrews made us to understand the serious consequences of Moses' disobedience in striking the rock instead of speaking to it. The bible revealed that the rock was Jesus and hence in a way, it was like crucifying the Savior twice although Jesus was to die once and for all.

For David, his theophanic encounter came when he was on the run from his rebellious son Absalom, during which he went through the same route and passage through which many years later great David's greater Son in the person of our Lord Jesus would go through on his way to the cross beginning from Gethsemane.

Unlike Moses, David, Joshua and other bible personages whose life, person and office has been used to typify God or his Coming Messiah, what is strange about the account of Melchizedek is the fact that nothing about his father, mother, descent nor ancestry was known. Similarly, the prophet Isaiah said about Jesus in Isaiah 53; that no one could declare his generation just as Melchizedek's generation and descent was unknown.

With Melchizedek the force of his figure lies in his background, etched in mystery and in the harsh surroundings of Canaan that is engulfed in a strong culture of heathenism. Though possessed with the knowledge of the Most-High God, his name is not found in any of those genealogies which show us how that knowledge passed from father to son. For All the other great men of the bible, their history are recorded and careful genealogy is given; but not Melchizedek.

There is something surprising and mysterious in the first appearance of Melchizedek on the scene momentarily with Abraham, and in the subsequent reference to him. He bore the title Priest of the Most-High God, which Jews in after ages would recognize as designating their own sovereign, as well as bearing gifts in the form of bread and wine which recall to Christians the Lord's Supper. [Smith's Bible Dictionary]

As a backdrop to the original encounter with Abram as recorded in the fourteenth chapter of Genesis; a band of men under Chedorlaomer carried away Lot (Abraham's nephew), along with other spoil, from Sodom. Abram, on learning this, armed his trained household, pursued the invaders, routed them, and set the captives free.

On his return, Melchizedek came out to meet him and to offer refreshment to Abram and his men; and as priest of his tribe and of the Most-High God, he blessed Abram. Whether the typology was understood by Abram or Melchizedek is not clear and matters not to us. What matters to us is the fact that these things are written for our learning and in them we see Christ bestowing his blessing.

All other references in the bible are references to this one occasion that he met with Abraham. So the big questions that this book will explore and attempt to answer about this strange figure are as follows:

1   Who was Melchizedek?

2   What are the ways in which Melchizedek's order of priesthood differs from the popular Aaronic (Levitical) priesthood?

3   How does the life, person and High-priestly office of Our Lord Jesus align with Melchizedek's order of priesthood?

4   Why should Melchizedek, and he alone, of all the Old Testament characters be thought of in a way that defiles human mortality?

Chapter 2

The Opinions about Melchizedek

To begin with, I would like to state all the scriptures in both the New and Old Testaments of the bible pertaining to Melchidezek. They aren't many scriptural references and they can be found in only three books of the bible, namely the book of Genesis where Melchizedek first appeared with Abraham and then references of that appearance in the Old Testament book of Psalm and the New Testament book of Hebrews.

Genesis 14: 17-23

(His original appearance of with Abraham)

17   And the king of Sodom went out to meet him after his return from the slaughter of Chedorlaomer, and of the kings that were with him, at the valley of Shaveh, which is the king's dale.

18   And Melchizedek king of Salem brought forth bread and wine: and he was the priest of the most-high God.

19   And he blessed him, and said, Blessed be Abram of the most high God, possessor of heaven and earth:

20   And blessed be the most high God, which hath delivered thine enemies into thy hand. And he gave him tithes of all.

21   And the king of Sodom said unto Abram, Give me the persons, and take the goods to thyself.

22 And Abram said to the king of Sodom, I have lift up mine hand unto the LORD, the most high God, the possessor of heaven and earth,

23 That I will not take from a thread even to a shoelatchet, † and that I will not take any thing that is thine, lest thou shouldest say, I have made Abram rich:

Psalm 110:1-4

(Old Testament Reference to Melchizedek)

"A Psalm of David. The LORD said unto my Lord, Sit thou at my right hand, until I make thine enemies thy footstool. †.

The LORD shall send the rod of thy strength out of Zion: rule thou in the midst of thine enemies.

Thy people shall be willing in the day of thy power, in the beauties of holiness from the womb of the morning: thou hast the dew of thy youth.

*The LORD hath sworn, and will not repent, Thou art a priest for ever after the order of **Melchizedek**."*

New Testament References to Melchizedek

Hebrews 5: 1-10

"For every high priest taken from among men is ordained for men in things pertaining to God, that he may offer both gifts and sacrifices for sins:

Who 'can' (not who will because only Jesus will) have compassion on the ignorant, and on them that are out of the way; for that he himself also is compassed with infirmity.

And by reason hereof he ought, as for the people, so also for himself, to offer for sins.

And no man taketh this honor unto himself, but he that is called of God, as was Aaron.

So also Christ glorified not himself to be made a high priest; but he that said unto him, Thou art my Son, to day have I begotten thee.

As he saith also in another place, Thou art a priest for ever after the order of **Melchisedec**.

Who in the days of his flesh, when he had offered up prayers and † supplications with strong crying and tears unto him that was able to save him from death, and was heard in that he feared;

Though he were a Son, yet learned he obedience by the things which he suffered;

And being made perfect, he became the author of eternal salvation unto all them that obey him;

Called of God an high priest after the order of Melchisedec."

Hebrew 6: 16-20

"For men verily swear by the greater: and an oath for confirmation is to them an end of all strife.

Wherein † God, willing more abundantly to shew unto the heirs of promise the immutability of his counsel, confirmed it by an oath:

That by two immutable things, in which it was impossible for God to lie, we might have a strong consolation, who have fled for refuge to lay hold upon the hope set before us:

Which hope we have as an anchor of the soul, both sure and stedfast, and which entereth into that within the veil;

*Whither the forerunner is for us entered, even Jesus, made an high priest for ever after the order of **Melchisedec**."*

Hebrew 7: 1-28

1 "For this Melchisedec, king of Salem, priest of the most high God, who met Abraham returning from the slaughter of the kings, and blessed him;

2 To whom also Abraham gave a tenth part of all; first being by interpretation King of righteousness, and after that also King of Salem, which is, King of peace;

3 Without father, without mother, without descent, having neither beginning of days, nor end of life; but made like unto the Son of God; abideth a priest continually. †.

4 Now consider how great this man was, unto whom even the patriarch Abraham gave the tenth of the spoils.

5 And verily they that are of the sons of Levi, who receive the office of the priesthood, have a commandment to take tithes of the people according to the law, that is, of their brethren, though they come out of the loins of Abraham:

6 But he whose descent is not counted from them received tithes of Abraham, and blessed him that had the promises.

7 And without all contradiction the less is blessed of the better.

8 And here † men that die receive tithes; but there he receiveth them, of whom it is witnessed that he liveth.

9 And as I may so say, † Levi also, who receiveth tithes, payed tithes in Abraham.

10 For he was yet in the loins of his father, when Melchisedec met him.

11 If † therefore perfection were by the Levitical priesthood, † (for under it the people received the law,) what further need was there that another priest should rise after the order of Melchisedec, and not be called after the order of Aaron?

12 For the priesthood being changed, there is made of necessity a change also of the law.

13 For he of whom these things are spoken pertaineth to another tribe, of which no man gave attendance at the altar.

14 For it is evident that our Lord sprang out of Juda; of which tribe Moses spake nothing concerning priesthood.

15 And it is yet far more evident: for that after the similitude of Melchisedec there ariseth another priest,

16 Who is made, not after the law of a carnal commandment, but after the power of an endless life.

17 For he testifieth, † Thou art a priest for ever after the order of Melchisedec.

18 For there is verily a disannulling of the commandment going before for the weakness and unprofitableness thereof.

19 For the law made nothing perfect, but the bringing in of a better hope did; by the which we draw nigh unto God.

20 And inasmuch as † not without an oath he was made priest:

21 (For those priests were made without an oath; but this with an oath by him that said unto him, The Lord sware and will not repent, Thou art a priest for ever after the order of Melchisedec:)

22 By so much was Jesus made a surety of a better testament.

23 And they truly were many priests, because they were not suffered to continue by reason of death:

24 But this man, because he continueth ever, hath an unchangeable priesthood.

25 Wherefore he is able also to save them to the uttermost that come unto God by him, seeing he ever liveth to make intercession for them.

26 For such an high priest became us, who is holy, harmless, undefiled, separate from sinners, and made higher than the heavens;

27 Who needeth not daily, as those high priests, to offer up sacrifice, first for his own sins, and then for the people's: for this he did once, when he offered up himself.

28 For the law maketh men high priests which have infirmity; but the word of the oath, which was since the law, maketh the Son, who is consecrated for evermore.

There have been various speculations as to who this Melchizedek was.

Shem

Some believed that he was Shem; the first and the best son of Noah. Shem was known to be the most important among the three sons of Noah. He was the one who inherited the greatest of his father's blessings and who also became the Lord of Canaan. He was made so by Noah according to **Genesis 9:25-26** *"And he said cursed be Canaan, a servant of servants shall he be to his brethren; And he said blessed be the Lord God of Shem and Canaan shall be his servant."*

It is possible that it could be Shem because we realize that Melchizedek is in Canaan, in Jerusalem which was the most important city in Canaan and of which the ancient name was Salem, as referenced to in Psalm 76:2. That's where God had directed Abraham to go and that's where Abraham in obedience to God's instruction had come.

It's also possible it could be Shem, as in those days people lived for very long years. Also, that some church historians held the view that Shem survived Abraham by forty years *[Pulpit Commentary Homiletics]*; However, this view is improbable because that would not apply which is stated of Melchizedek, in **Hebrews 7:3** - that he was *"without father, without mother, without descent, having neither beginning of days, nor end of life; but made like unto the Son of God; abideth a priest continually."*

> *"We do know the ancestry of Shem, and we also know who his father and mother and brethren are from the bible but not that of Melchizedek"* [PCH;Pulpit Commentary Homiletics"]

Notice also that we get our word Semitism from Shem and anti-Semitism, which means *anti-Shem-ism* (or anti the descendants of Shem) and by the way who are the descendants of Shem? The most important and most prominent descendants among the Semitic race (Descendants of Shem) we know of are the children of Israel. That's why the word anti-Semitism (anti-Shem) is used in reference to hatred directed towards the Jewish people.

Angel

Some have thought that Melchizedek was an angel sent from God to minister to Abraham on his return from battle. Chief among those who held this view was the Church Historian Origen.

Superior Intercessor

Some believed that Melchizedek was a superior being to Christ and that he was an intercessor for the angels just like Jesus Christ was an intercessor for humans. As you can see, this particular view is obviously far-fetched from the views of mainstream Christianity hence I would not dwell on it.

Jewish Tradition

Some Jews have also held that Melchizedek was the first appearance of the Messiah because they held a long standing tradition that the Messiah will appear in:

1   Manifested power and glory and then
2   He will appear in poverty and lowliness

They are right in that the Messiah will first appear in shame and lowliness and then later, return in power and glory because this is the Christian view and that's what we believe as Christians. This position is supported by the fact that there are so many scriptures in the bible that reveal that the Messiah will come in poverty. For example as in **Isaiah 53:2-3** *"...he hath no form nor comeliness; and when we shall see him, there is no beauty that we should desire of him 3)He is despised and rejected of men; a man of sorrows, and acquainted with grief...."*

In like manner, there are also so many scriptures that reveal that the Messiah will come in glory. Particularly, in the book of Isaiah and in many of the Messianic Psalms, such as Psalms 24, 71, 79.

Therefore when we are approaching Jews we shouldn't argue with them concerning the coming of the Messiah because both Christians and Jews believe that the Messiah will come in shame and poverty and then in power and glory.

The only difference between the Jewish and Christian views about the Messiah is that Christians believe when he comes in power and glory it will be the second time whereas Jews believe that will be his first time.

Other Opinions

Others have held that Melchizedek was a manifestation of Christ being the pre-incarnation of Our Lord Jesus Christ (Ambrose), which is contrary to Hebrews 6:20. If so, Christ would have been the type and the antitype. We are aware that Christ manifested himself in Old Testament days - it was called a *'Christophany.'* Christophany therefore is a manifestation of the coming Christ or Messiah in human form. *'Theophany'* on the other hand is a manifestation of God in human form.

> As Christians we believe that every Christophany is also a Theophany because the Father and the Son; they are one.

Jesus said to his disciples when they asked him to show them the Father; *"he that hath seen me hath seen the father because he is in me and I in him,"* furthermore in another reference as in **John 10; 30** he said again that *"I and my father are one."*

When God appeared unto Moses, it was a Christophany and when God appeared unto Abraham, it was a Theophany because three angels appeared unto Abraham, and two went towards Sodom but the other remained and the one which remained is God for God takes delight in being with his Children.

So many believe Melchizedek was a manifestation of the Coming Christ to Abraham which will make it a *Christophany*

Some believed that Melchizedek was Enoch who had returned back to earth since he was one of the only two people in the bible who did not experience death and who possibly lived closest to the time of Abraham as compared to Elijah. Others has said Melchizedek was Japheth, or Job the tried one, or Canaan the cursed grandson of Noah etc. But these are all speculations which does not have full support of scriptures and to say the least is quite difficult to harmonize with what the book of Hebrews has to say about Melchizedek.

Today we have very few preachers who unfold scripture; instead what we have are preachers who use the scriptures to support their opinions or some ideas about scriptural truths.

In this book, instead of using the scriptures to support an idea, I will rather unfold the truth of scripture without using it to support any preconceived theological concept. So let's see what the bible has to say about this great one Melchizedek. Who was he?

Chapter 3

Melchizedek – Who Was He?

It is quite clear that Melchizedek could not have been Shem the first Son of Noah.

This is because the bible said *"he is without Father and without Mother, nor descent; he is without beginning of days or end of life";*

In other words, he had no known genealogy. We know the mother and father of Shem and we know of all his brothers and descendants. For each of the Patriarch s we can tell their paternity; the time of their birth, if not their death; but this man Melchizedek, stands alone with none to claim him.

"Shem could not be Melchizedek because; it is unlikely that a man whose pedigree was distinctly known should have been selected as typical instance of a man whose pedigree was altogether unknown"

[PCH;Pulpit Commentary Homiletics]

Melchizedek could not be the Lord Jesus Christ either.

This is because it said in the book of Hebrews that *"he was made like unto the Lord Jesus Christ;"* **Hebrews 7:3b.**

I will admonish you when you study the bible to ask God to give you what I call, 'sanctified common sense' because, you there is no way that you can be like me and be me at the same time. If one person is like another person obviously they are two separate individuals and not one.

Melchizedek forms no part of any series of links by which the past and the present times are connected

---

So as he is made like unto the Lord Jesus Christ; this means that he could not be the Lord Jesus Christ. What else may we know about him?

That he is of the race of the people among whom we find him. That is, he is a Canaanite.

Melchizedek appears to be greatly respected;

His name Melchizedek is derived from (*malchi*) meaning "my king" and *(zedek) meaning* "is righteousness." Hence by putting the two parts of his name together, his name means "My King is Righteous or My Lord is Righteous." It's more of a title than a real name. '*Zedek*' may have been a title adopted by a line of kings of Canaan, or it may have been peculiar to this one man Melchizedek, we are not sure. But these old Canaanites, had certainly got hold of a great principle when they gave this title to the king of their city of Salem or Peace.

Later on in Joshua 10:1-4 at the time when Joshua led the children of Israel to conquer Canaan, we hear of another King of Jerusalem who was known as; Adonai-zedek (God of justice).

Joshua 10:1-4 *"Now it came to pass, when Adonizedec king of Jerusalem had heard how Joshua had taken Ai, and had utterly destroyed it; as he had done to Jericho and her king, so he* *had done to Ai and her king; and how the inhabitants of Gibeon had made peace with Israel, and were among them;*

2 That they feared greatly, because Gibeon was a great city, as one of the royal cities, and because it was greater than Ai, and all the men thereof were mighty.

3 Wherefore Adonizedec king of Jerusalem, sent unto Hoham king of Hebron, and unto Piram king of Jarmuth, and unto Japhia king of Lachish, and unto Debir king of Eglon, saying,

4 Come up unto me, and help me, that we may smite Gibeon: for it hath made peace with Joshua and with the children of Israel.

Adonai-zedek unlike Melchi-zedek, lacked spiritual wisdom and understanding, hence instead of welcoming the descendants of Shem (the children of Israel) whom Melchizedek welcomed in the person of Abraham and gave him gifts, he instead became fearful and organized an attack against them.

It is also interesting to note that Archaeologist discovered in the south of Palestine, a tablet (i.e. among the Tell el-Amarna Letters), among which are at least six letters from a king of Urusalim (identified with and translated as Jerusalem) saying to his Egyptian Overlord Amenophis IV, King of Egypt, whose "slave" the former calls himself. The name of this king is given as Abd-chiba (pronounced as Abdi-taba), who is believed to be the successor of Adoni-zedek who is also believed to be a successor of Melchi-zedek.

In these letters, three times are found the statement in which the King of Jerusalem many hundreds of years after Melchizedek, tells his Egyptian overlord, "Neither my father nor my mother set me in this place but the arm of the mighty king established me in my father's house"

(Letter 102 in Berlin collection, ll. 9-13; also number 103, ll. 25-28; number 104, ll. 13-15).

We have no actual proof that Melchizedek is identical with Abdi-taba; possibly the reference to the former as being "without father," etc., is not to be explained as above. However, notice the similarity of Abdi-taba's statement to the very words that described Melchizedek as being; *"Without Father, Without mother, without decent of days."*

In other words, this Abdi-taba a heathen King of Jerusalem was saying that he was not put into office by any human being; nor by right of decent, but the most high God put him there. That he arrived at this office not by descent through my Mother or my Father. The words meant originally that he acknowledged that he did not come to the throne because he had a claim on it through descent; God confirmed it in the Psalm 48 by saying, this is the city of the great king.

Psalm 48:1-2 [A Song *and* Psalm for the sons of Korah.]

1   "Great is the LORD, and greatly to be praised in the city of our God, in the mountain of his holiness.

2   Beautiful for situation, the joy of the whole earth, is mount Zion, on the sides of the north, the city of the great King."

Melchizedek seem to be respected for his Holy, Kingly, Priestly and Prophetic character.

Never make the mistake to believe that God confines his revelation only to Israel or to the Jewish people alone. God had given revelation to people of many other races outside the Jewish nation.

It's true that God gave the major revelation to the people from among who will come the Messiah; but he also gave minor revelation of himself to people of other race. For an example, Job who was one of God's best was not a Jew. The bible made us know that Job was the richest among the men of the East; that's not Palestine but rather the 'East' refers to Arabia. And now comes Melchizedek; not a Jew of course; a Canaanite.

> "There was something very mysterious and at the same time typical in the person, name, office, residence and governance of this Canaanitish Priest"
>
> [Clarke's Commentary]

There may be so many others that we know of from the bible and some that we don't even know of that God may have revealed himself to them. Otherwise he could not judge them, if he had not given them any revelation of himself.

> While all our attention is concentrated on Abram as carrying the whole spiritual hope of the world, there emerges from an obscure Canaanite valley a man nearer to God than Abram.

Therefore, even in Canaan and among their heathenism and anti-God culture, before Abraham even got there; here is a man who is a priest, King, and Prophet of the most-high God and of worshippers of the one true God in Canaan. His life was like a bright star shining amid the general heathenism of Canaan. I guess this is because God does not put all his eggs in one basket as the saying goes. This saying, as humorous as it is, may very well be the case because some very notable personages in the Bible were not Jews and yet they were mightily used of God. An example is Rahab the harlot, and a citizen of Jericho who after hundreds of years after hosting the spies from Israel, was named among the few women in the genealogy of our Lord Jesus. So is Ruth the Moabitess, Job, Melchizedek, the Gibeonites and many others.

Melchizedek was the King of righteousness and Priest of the Most-High God at the same time. King-Priest was well known among the nations even before the nation of Israel was formed. Abraham was a Patriarch and a priest of his family and so was Isaac, Jacob, Enoch, Job, Jethro, Balaam and many others. The Patriarch offered sacrifices unto God on behalf of his family. We see also even in the Garden of Eden where Abel and Cain were offering sacrifices. Job also offered sacrifices for his family peradventure his children in making merry may have sinned against God.

> The office of the priesthood did not start with Aaron because even before God instituted the Aaronic priesthood, there is record of sacrifices made unto God.

Also before the Aaronic priesthood; there was this tradition where the King was also the priest and the prophet at the same time. However, under the Jewish dispensation there was no one who in his person could represent the twofold character of Christ as the only High Priest and universal King. The Levitical priesthood could not supply a perfect type, for it had no one who was fit to serve simultaneously in the office of priest and king. Not even Moses the great leader and pastor of the flock of Israel could claim both offices.

As we know God split that office between Moses and Aaron whereby Moses was the leader and Aaron the priest. David in his time ventured not to interfere with the priestly office. Likewise, Solomon, at the dedication of the temple, when he blessed the people, gave sacrifices for the priests to offer, King Uzziah on the contrary attempted to intrude into the priestly office at the same time that he was king, but ended up being stricken with leprosy by God.

Under the patriarchal dispensation and in Melchizedek there is this very plain type of Christ in his priestly and kingly character. God was the Most-High God to Melchizedek and Almighty with the Patriarch. He is Jehovah with Israel, and will be Most High God again during the millennium.

For this reason, the Roman rulers of old were known as Pontifex Maximus; consequently we would see on the Roman coin the inscription; 'Pont Max; which is abbreviation for Pontifex Maximus. When the Roman Empire collapsed, the head of the Roman Catholic Church took on the title as the Pontifex Maximus; that's why even until today the Pope is referred to as the Supreme Pontiff. That was until God stopped it and established a new order with a Kingship that was separate from the priesthood in Israel.

A pontiff (from Latin *pontifex*) was, in Roman antiquity, a member of the most illustrious of the colleges of priests of the Roman religion, the College of Pontiffs. The term "pontiff" was later applied to any high or chief priest and in Roman Catholic ecclesiastical usage, to a bishop and more particularly to the Bishop of Rome, the Pope or "Roman Pontiff" **[The American Heritage Dictionary of the English Language]**

Chapter 4

The Order of Melchizedek and of Our Lord Jesus

Far before Christ was born, the bible made us know with all surety that the high priestly office of our Lord Jesus was to follow the order of Melchizedek's priesthood. So, in what ways could the priesthood of Melchizedek be aligned to that of our Lord Jesus and what exactly are the parallels and typology.

Melchizedek appears on the stage of the bible for one divine purpose; to reveal to us how the priesthood of the coming Christ that will last forever will be. After that, he is quickly taken off the scene.

Both were priest of the Most High God.

Bible references to Melchizedek's office indicate that it was without definite beginning or ending. The Levitical priesthood had a definite beginning and ending; that of Melchizedek never ended. One stood in carnal ceremonies, while the other in the power of an a holy character and an endless life. Jesus became a priest when he entered heaven by his own blood Hebrews 8:1-4, Hebrews 10:11-12. His priesthood is independent of the Aaronic priesthood as it's known that he is from the tribe of Judah of which Moses said nothing about the priesthood. He had no predecessor, and he will have no successor. He will remain in heaven and officiate as priest until such a time that the work of redemption is done.

Both were priest by direct institution - not through a priestly line.

When the bible says; *"Melchizedek was without descent nor without father and mother"*; it does not mean he has no father or mother. What is means is that, he comes unto the scene without any revelation of who his father or mother was; and goes off the scene without any further clue to the same.

For as Melchizedek stands thus on the page of history, so is Our Lord Jesus in reality. As the one has no recorded pedigree, and holds an office beginning and ending in his own person.

None could say Melchizedek was their father and there was none that could say Melchizedek was their son; not to say he has no heirs; but that does not come into the picture as far as what God wanted to use his life to teach us is concern.

And so God brings Melchizedek on the scene as a living King, a living priest, and a living prophet and takes him off the scene as a living king, priest and prophet.

The reason being that if the first and old covenant was temporal and faulty according to the bible, then there is the need for a new covenant of which we (New Testament Believers) are a part and which is made not after the order of the Levitical priesthood but rather after the order of Melchizedek since it will stand forever.

God is bringing Melchizedek into the picture; to teach us that like Melchizedek, Christ has no earthly descent.

Christ's nature was derived directly from the God-head. He only took upon him a human form. The words of the apostle Paul in **Hebrew 7:3**, state only that the sacred history the bible has said nothing of his ancestors.

The silence of the Scriptures on Our Lord Jesus' descent, is to raise our thoughts to Him, whose generation cannot be declared.

This is why **Isaiah 53:8** asserts that, *"He was taken from prison and from judgment: and who shall declare his generation...?"*

The omissions concerning parentage or the beginning of his priesthood were probably designed by God in order to convey to us, what would be the characteristics of the order of his High-priestly office to which Christ would later follow. This would then explain the force of the prophecy in Psalm 110 and the plain words of the Apostle Paul in Hebrews 7.

So our Lord, though born of a woman, stands separate from sinners and quite out of the ordinary line of generations, and exercises an office which he received hereditarily from none, and which he could commit to no successor.

He is God who took upon himself a human form; he is not human who became divine. (Please note the difference once and for all). Like us, we are flesh who acquired divinity as a gift from God; but Christ on the other hand is God taking on flesh that's why Isaiah said *"Unto us a child is born; unto us a Son is given."*

While the child is 'born' because he is the human baby Jesus, the Son on the other hand is not born; He is 'given' because the Son is one with God and God cannot be born seeing he is eternal.

Melchizedek did not inherit his priesthood office from an ancestor and neither passed on the office to anyone.

The third verse of the seventh chapter of Hebrews, probably means merely this - that his descent was not known, and that his priesthood was not inherited or derived from others, but rather one resting in his individual character. *[PCH; Pulpit Commentary Homiletics]*.

Similarly is Our Lord Jesus obviously by his genealogy, did not come out of the priestly line of Levi in order to inherit the priesthood; he came from Judah of which according to the book of Hebrews, Moses said nothing about the Priesthood.

John the Baptist on the other hand was a priest and the last of the prophets because he was of the line of the Levitical priesthood. His father was a priest and he inherited the priesthood from his father but Jesus was not a Levite; he was from the tribe of Judah of which God said nothing about the priesthood.

That's why the bible says of Jesus in the book of Hebrews that; *"he remains a priest continual after the order of Melchizedek." Obviously because, his priesthood could not conform to the order of the Levitical priesthood.*

Continual: *means he is priest for an unlimited time but it does not mean his priesthood office is limitless.*

What this means is that he is a priest as long as God would want him to be a priest and that no one has the power to revoke or annul his priesthood or destroy that priesthood. In a manner that's just like us; whatever God has purposed to do in your life; no demon or devil in hell can alter God's purposes in your life. Will they try? Oh yes they will but they will not succeed.

Melchizedek was superior to Abraham; and so was Christ.

Jesus once said to his audience;

"Before Abraham was, I am" said Christ.

and his audience were ready to stone him because they claimed that what he said was blasphemous seeing he was not even 50 years of age and father Abraham lived hundreds and hundreds of years before Christ. Then as if to add insult to injury, Christ added that; *"I knew Abraham; Abraham rejoice to see my days."* In other words; Abraham knew I was coming and was glad about my coming.

So here is this great Abraham paying tithes to Melchizedek; He did it for one reason, which is to show Melchizedek's superiority to him. Here is Abraham, the friend of God; the man into whose bosom all the righteous souls who died were comforted until Christ rose again from the dead and confronted the gates of hell. Abraham whose seed as an earthly seed will be more than the sand at the shore and whose heavenly seed of which we are a part will be more than the stars of heaven, comes on the scene paying tithes to another man. The great Patriarch Abraham who is the father of two kinds of seed. That is an earthly seed which comprise of Israel and Ishmael and a celestial seed or heavenly seed which comprise of all the children of Faith in all generations after him as the scripture says is seem paying tithes to a greater who is Melchizedek.

As Melchizedek stands apparently disconnected from all before and after him, so Jesus thus suddenly emerge from eternity, owning the authority of earthly parents, yet claiming an antiquity greater than Abram's.

That's why the bible says we are the children of Abraham and Abraham is our father when we have the faith of Abraham. Yet this great man Abraham recognizes the superiority of Melchizedek and paid him tithes. He in receiving tithes from Abram, shows his superiority over Abraham because according to **Hebrews 7:7** the *'lesser is blessed of the greater"* hence the receiver is greater than the giver of tithe. I would therefore strongly encourage you to be faithful in tithing to your local church because the same principle underlies the paying of tithes in our churches today. It secures the blessing of the lesser (you) by the greater (God).

"By taking precedence of Abram and blessing him, and receiving of him tithes, he became the representative of a higher priesthood than that which could spring from Abram's loins in the form of the Levitical priesthood"

[Ellicott's Commentary for English Readers]

But it was not so with Abraham's grandson Jacob; when he met the Great Pharaoh of Egypt who was the head of the greatest empire the world had ever seen in those days. Pharaoh said unto Jacob, how old art thou and in response Jacob said "few and evil have the days of the years of my life been, and have not attained unto the days of the years of the life of my fathers in the days of their pilgrimage" **Genesis 47:9** And in the next verse, we are told Jacob blessed Pharaoh and went out from before Pharaoh. This is opposite to Abraham's encounter with Melchizedek because here; *"the greater, who is Pharaoh is blessed of the lesser who is Jacob"* but in the case of Abraham; he being the lesser is being blessed by Melchizedek who is the greater. That's how Great Melchizedek was.

It was said in the book of Hebrew that Melchizedek was the priest of the *"Most High God."* A term which before that hasn't been ever used "the Most High God"

So, here in the land of Canaan, there are worshippers of the Most High God who look to Melchizedek as their priest. In like manner today, so must all who worship God come to him through their Great High Priest our Lord Jesus Christ.

Jesus unlike any spiritual leader ever before or after him, boldly proclaim the following as recorded in **John 14:6** *"I am the way, truth and the life; no man cometh unto the Father but by me."*

Melchizedek was not appointed only for a period of time; he was supposed to be a priest for all the days of his life: And so is Christ.

"Thou art a priest forever after the order of Melchizedek."

This does not mean that he is appointed a priest for a limitless time; but he is a priest for all the time God wanted him to be a priest unto his people. And so is Christ; **Hebrews 7** *"he abideth a priest forever continually after the order of Melchizedek."*

Continual not in the sense of never ending but rather in the sense of being indestructible; meaning, no one can put him out of the priesthood. The Aaronic priesthood was often interrupted by death. Christ is a priest after the order of Melchizedek, as King of righteousness, King of peace Isaiah 11:4-9, Hebrews 7:2 and in the endlessness of his priesthood.

When God appoints one to do a work not even the forces of darkness or the gates of Hell shall be able to prevail against the will and purpose of God. So you need not burst the door open or push on the window. In other words, don't exercise unholy rush in order to achieve anything. Simply wait upon the Lord and again I say wait; because whatever God want to do in your life He will do; and whatever God doesn't want you to do, don't even try doing. Stop pushing yourself on a popularity campaign. Instead, rest in the Lord and enjoy the abiding peace that the Holy Spirit brings to obedient Kingdom sons or daughters. God will certainly bring to pass what he said he will do in your life.

Christ like Melchizedek is priest forever; therefore as long as God want him to be priest He will be priest.

Make no mistake-there is nothing in scripture that suggests that Christ is for evermore a priest.

According to I Cor. 11:3 *"But I would have you know, that the head of every man is Christ; and the head of the woman is the man; and the head of Christ is God."*

This means that Christ is equal with the father in power, authority and judgment but he voluntary and gladly acknowledged the father's headship.

"As Christ is equal with God, so the church is equal with Christ but acknowledged his Lordship; and so is the woman equal with the man but acknowledges his Leadership"

Amid Christ and God, there is a perfect equality. Christ thought it not robbery to be equal with God because he is God. As Christ is equal with God, so the church is equal with Christ but acknowledges his Lordship; and so is the woman equal with the man but acknowledges not his Lordship but rather his Leadership.

So when you hear people quote that *"the head of the woman is the man and the head of the man is Christ...etc."* they most often never finish the quotation because most often these domineering men whether they are Christians or not, quote this scripture with the mentality of the man being a "Boss" over the woman.

If you look at the complete picture, you will see that there is no 'bossing' among the parties here, whether is between Christ and God, or the man and the woman; because the equality that exist between Christ and God is the same that is passed on to the relationship between the man and the woman. If God is not the boss over Christ then in like manner the man is not the boss over the woman.

It goes on to say that; and the Head of Christ is God. So there is a perfect sweet communion between the two.

The man in his role as the leader does not mean he is a boss, but rather the one who:

- Takes responsibility,
- Carries the weight,
- Who provides for his family,
- And also as the one who takes the blame when things go wrong

Let's look at **I Corinthians 15:22-28** where it reveals that just like Melchizedek, Christ's priesthood office will last as long as the father would allow it to after which it will come to an end.

22 For as in Adam all die, even so in Christ shall all be made alive.

"When one refers to women taking their rightful place it does not mean they should be subjects, servants or slaves to the man but rather it means they are equal with the man just like Christ is equal with God, while acknowledging the man as the leader"

23   But every man in his own order: Christ the firstfruits; afterward they that are Christ's at his coming.

24   Then cometh the end, when he (JESUS) shall have delivered up the kingdom to God, even the Father; when he shall have put down all rule and all authority and power.

25   For he must reign, till he hath put all enemies under his feet. 26) The last enemy that shall be destroyed is death.

26   For he (GOD) hath put all things under his (JESUS) feet. But when he saith all things are put under him, it is manifest that he is excepted, which did put all things under him.

27   And when all things shall be subdued unto him, then shall the Son also himself be subject unto him (God) that put all things under him, that God may be all in all.

The subjection of the Son to the Father as stated in the verse 28 above, does not in any way make the Son inferior to the Father. The implication here is that; the intercessory high-priestly office of the Son would then come to an end when there is no more need for him to intercede on our behalf as our great High-Priest.

So Christ eventually is to give up his high-priestly capacity. This will occur when the need for Christ as our intercessor comes to an end, in that moment he will seize to intercede. But presently he intercedes for every one of us with groaning that cannot be uttered because. He is the great intercessor who ever lives to make intercession for us, and the one who saves to the uttermost, all who come unto the Father by him.

This is a sweet subjection of two equals, one to the other; a holy communion between two equals.

Chapter 5

Melchizedek, King of Salem, King of Righteousness & Priest of the Most-High

Referencing back to the original text in Genesis 14; we read that *"Melchizedek is King of Salem."*

He is king and simultaneously a priest. His name means, king of righteousness. He dwells in Salem, which is by interpretation is the place of peace. That's one of the great greetings that our Lord Jesus who is also King of peace like to use. When he saw the disciples at the shore after his death; he said to them 'peace unto you.'

Luke 24:36 (KJV)

36 "And as they thus spake, Jesus himself stood in the midst of them, and saith unto them, Peace be unto you."

When he appeared unto them while they were fearful and in hiding from the Jewish authorities; he said unto them in John 20:19 (KJV)

19 "Then the same day at evening, being the first day of the week, when the doors were shut where the disciples were assembled for

> fear of the Jews, came Jesus and stood in the midst, and saith unto
> them, Peace be unto you."

Also eight days after his resurrection Jesus appeared unto
his disciples as recorded in John 20:26 and said;

> 26 "And after eight days again his disciples were within, and Thom-
> as with them: then came Jesus, the doors being shut, and stood in
> the midst, and said, Peace be unto you."

As one of his last words of comfort to his fearful disciples,
Jesus encouraged them with these words as stated in John
14:27 (KJV)

> 27 "Peace I leave with you, my peace I give unto you: not as the
> world giveth, give I unto you. Let not your heart be troubled,
> neither let it be afraid."

Lastly, and before he gave them the great charge and sent
them out to spread the good news that his death, burial and
resurrection brings to humanity, he said unto them in John
20:21(KJV)

> 21 "Then said Jesus to them again, Peace be unto you: as my Father
> hath sent me, even so send I you."

Why all these salutations about peace? It is because like
Melchizedek, Our Lord Jesus is also King of Salem, which
is the same as 'Shalom' and which by interpretation means
'peace be unto you.' Like Melchizedek, Christ is King of
Peace (King of Salem) that's why at his birth the angels who
announced the birth of Christ added that peace has come on
earth as a result of his birth.

Christ is called the Prince of peace, because, by his incarnation, sacrifice and mediation, he procures and establishes peace between God and man. Besides, he heals the breaches and dissensions between heaven and earth, reconciling both; and produces glory to God in the highest, and on earth peace and good will among men as declared at his birth by the angel. His residence is peace and quietness and assurance forever, for every believing upright heart. He governs as the Prince of Peace and as the Priest of the most-high God, ruling in righteousness and mighty to save.

Salem means possession of peace and this is made very clear in Psalm 76 which declares that;

Psalm 76:1-2; *In **Judah** is God known: his name is great in **Israel**.*

2 *"In Salem also is his tabernacle, and his dwelling place in Zion."*

Psalm 76 also makes it clear that Zion and Salem are the same. Salem is "Jeru-salem."

It is worth noting that even after David and the people of Israel inhabited Jerusalem; there were pockets of Zionites which dwell in the mountains on the outskirts of Jerusalem. It was David who finally conquered the city of Zion which the Zionites have considered impregnable; they had said that even the strongest of nations cannot take down their fortified city and David said they could.

That's what the bible was referring to when it says in II **Sam 5:3-7.** that "after David was anointed King over Judah first and then over Israel; he took down the stronghold of Zion."

"So all the elders of Israel came to the king to Hebron; and king David made a league with them in Hebron before the Lord: and they anointed David king over Israel.

4   David was thirty years old when he began to reign, and he reigned forty years.

5   In Hebron he reigned over Judah seven years and six months: and in Jerusalem he reigned thirty and three years over all Israel and Judah.

6   And the king and his men went to Jerusalem unto the Jebusites, the inhabitants of the land: which spake unto David, saying, Except thou take away the blind and the lame, thou shalt not come in hither: thinking, David cannot come in hither.

7   Nevertheless David took the strong hold of Zion: the same is the city of David."

So after David's penetration into the stronghold of Zion, Zion became identical with Jerusalem. So listen to what the Psalmist says about Zion in Psalm 48; 1-2.

Psalm 48:1-2 1) *Great is the Lord, and greatly to be praised in the city of our God, in the mountain of his holiness.*

2   "Beautiful for situation, the joy of the whole earth, is mount Zion, on the sides of the north, the city of the great King."

This man Melchizedek was a priest but offered no sacrifices; He is a type of the Most High Priest Our Lord Jesus.

That is just like Christ who although a high Priest after the order of Melchizedek, who would not offer earthly sacrifices with the blood of bulls and goats in conformance with the practices of the Levitical priesthood. But would only offer one sacrifice for sins forever with his own blood and then sit down on the right-hand of the father above.

It is clear that Melchizedek offers no sacrifice but he blesses Abraham without it. So is Our Lord Jesus who offered no sacrifice with the blood of bulls and goats as demanded by the priestly office under the Aaronic priesthood yet blesses us with all heavenly blessing without it.

Listen to what Hebrews 7: 27-28 says about that.

Hebrew 7:27 *"**Who needeth not daily, as those high priests, to offer up sacrifice,** first for his own sins, and then for the people's: **for this he did once, when he offered up himself**."*

> 28   For the law maketh men high priests which have infirmity; but the word of the oath, which was since the law, maketh the Son, who is consecrated for evermore."

Unconsecrated though he was, Jesus became the source of consecration.

Psalm. 110:4 makes very clear *'the word of the oath'* referred to in Hebrew 7:28 above.

Psalm 110:4 *"The Lord hath **sworn**, and will not repent, Thou art a priest for ever after the order of Melchizedek."*

The words of *Psalm 110:4* are taken to refer to Him *Hebrews 5:5*, and in *Hebrews 7:5* the order of Melchizedek is held to be higher than that of the Aaronic order of priesthood, that is why the superiority of Melchizedek was acknowledged by Abraham. First by paying tithes to Melchizedek and secondly when he was blessed by Melchizedek, for "the less is blessed of the better." **[International Standard Bible Encyclopedia]**

And so we see that Melchizedek blesses Abraham, but the blessing was not merely wishing Abraham good luck. When a greater blesses a lesser it is entirely different from when a lesser blesses the greater. When a greater blesses a lesser, real blessings goes along with it. The blessing is accompanied by an impartation of unction and an anointing. *The blessing of the Lord maketh rich and added no sorrow to it.* **Proverbs 10:22.**

For example, when God who is greater blesses you the lesser, he is not wishing you good luck or saying some sweet words in your ears, no not at all. The blessings of the Lord carry heavy weight with it. You are destined to receive something out of that blessing and his glory and favor comes down upon your life as a result of it. That's what Abraham received when he was blessed of the Lord through Melchizedek. He got the blessing of the Most High God through being blessed by Melchizedek. It was bestowed upon him as an unction.

Like Abraham, when you are truly blessed by the greater, earthly riches would not mean much to you.

Let's see what happens after Abraham received this blessing. After he was blessed by Melchizedek, Abraham could now despise earthly riches.

As a result of being blessed by a greater (Melchizedek), Abraham was offered riches by the King of Sodom and he refused the offer. The King of Sodom said to Abraham; *"you give me all the people you have rescued and take all the riches and the spoil* and Abraham said to the king of Sodom – *"I have lifted up mine hand unto the Lord that I will not take even a thread nor a shoe latchet from you lest you may say you have made me rich."*

Abraham was only able to say that because he highly esteemed the blessings of the greater (Melchizedek) far above the blessing of the lesser (King of Sodom). In other words, he was saying that if he is blessed of God, what else could the King of Sodom add to that blessing that would make him any better?

It is interesting to note that Abram bows himself before Melchizedek, but before the king of Sodom he lifts his hand. Thus Abram recognizes and acknowledges Melchizedek, while he penetrates to its depth the nature of the king of Sodom. **[Lange Commentary on the Holy Scriptures]**

"To lift ones hands up unto the Lord," is both a gesture of praying and of swearing. So with the riches of heavenly blessings on his life, he could despise earthly riches from the King of Sodom, and because his heart was free from the attachment to riches of this world, God could really bless him with greater riches which extends to his posterity, the descendants of Shem.

When Moses found himself in a similar position where he had to choose between the riches that Pharaoh's Palace offered as compared to the blessings and joy that suffering with the people of God and abiding under the will of God brings, his choice was very clear as stated in **Hebrews 11:24-27.**

24 "By faith Moses, when he was come to years, refused to be called the son of Pharaoh's daughter;

25 Choosing rather to suffer affliction with the people of God, than to enjoy the pleasures of sin for a season;

26 Esteeming the reproach of Christ greater riches than the treasures in Egypt: for he had respect unto the recompence of the reward.

27 By faith he forsook Egypt, not fearing the wrath of the king: for he endured, as seeing him who is invisible."

How can we really say that God gave the success when we are willing to pursue human measures of success, using man-centered wisdom and methods?

For some people their attachment to their little earthly possessions has driven them away from greater life and blessing in the Lord. As a result, some are left poor and miserable on the inside; yet are trying to show greatness on the outside. This is just in line with what people from the Island of Jamaica rightly label *"poor show great."* They are poor and miserable on the inside but pretend on the outside that all is well with them.

It is much better to follow God's wisdom so that when success comes God gets the glory, and it is evident to everyone that it is the doing of the Lord. Therefore, after he was been blessed by Melchizedek; Abraham could now refer to God by the term - *The Most High God*. This is the first account in the bible that this term has been used of the *"Most high God."*

Literally, meaning *El-Elyon* in the Hebrew and it's a proper name for the Supreme Deity, occurring only here, in the narrative of Abram's interview with the kings and of which the first term, *El*, from the same root as Elohim (Genesis 1:1), signifies the Strong One. It is seldom applied to God without some qualifying attribute as in *El-Shaddai*, or *El*, the God of Israel; The second part, 'Elion occurred frequently afterwards, as in *Numbers 24:16; Deuteronomy 32:8;* and in some messianic Psalms as in *Psalm 7:18, Psalm 7:17, Psalms 9:2* which describes God as the Highest, the Exalted, the Supreme. [Pulpit Commentary].

It is interesting to note that the same reference to God is made in the New Testament again and on no other occasion than on the occasion of the announcement of the birth of Christ who is the everlasting King of peace and King of Righteousness.

"El-Elyon speaks of the absolute pre-eminence of God. It also speaks of His absolute perfection in himself, and his sovereign dominion over all creation."

[Wesley's Notes on the Bible]

Luke 2; 13-14 *"And suddenly there appeared with the angel a great multitude of the heavenly host, praising God and saying: glory to **God in the highest."***

'Glory to God in the Highest',is exactly the same as *"The Most High God"*

Isn't it wonderful to know that *El-Elyon* (The Most High God) is your habitation and your provider?

Chapter 6

The Spiritual Significance of Melchizedek's Appearance with Abraham

Melchizedek Appear on the Scene and Gave Gifts

After Abraham's battle with the *band of men under Chedorlaomer,* Melchizedek appeared on the scene with his hands full of gifts for Abraham and blessed him. Our Lord Jesus also, being the antitype of Melchizedek, and as King of peace (Isaiah 9:6; cf. Luke 2:14; John 14:27) appeared suddenly to lead captivity captive, with His hands full of gifts, and His lips dropping words of blessing according to Ephesians 4:

Ephesians 4:8 *"Wherefore he saith, when he ascended up on high, he led captivity captive, and gave gifts unto men."*

What Kind of Gift?

Melchizedek served Abram with **bread and wine**; and when the Lord Jesus blessed his disciples on earth during the last supper and before his crucifixion; what did he give them?

He served them the same bread and wine as of the Passover and the Lord's Table. Take a look at our redeeming sacrifice, Jesus Christ.

By Melchizedek, offering bread and wine to Abraham, we can't help but to think of the Lord's Supper in which Our Lord Jesus offered bread and wine to his disciples.

Jesus said the bread is His body and the wine representing His blood; therefore we can't help thinking about the Lord's Supper. That tells us that indeed Jesus is the bread of heaven and we feed on him with thanksgiving. It is therefore about time we take a fresh look at the attitude with which we approach the Lord's Table during communion services.

As an illustration of the importance of coming together to dine at the Lord's table during communion services; let us reflect upon the good times we have shared with family members. One would realize that our memories often settle upon the time spend at the dinner table during family meals. This is because when we sit at the dinner table with one another, we not only share food, but also our lives. If therefore a sacrament is "an actual conveyance of spiritual meaning and power by a material process" then it means partaking of the Lord's table entwines the material and the spiritual in a remarkable way. The bread and wine in and of itself is purely physical, but it represents the body and blood of Jesus the efficacious Lamb of God.

When we realize how deeply a meal together can be a spiritual and regenerating experience, we can understand something of why our Lord Jesus, when he broke bread with his disciples toward the end of their earthly fellowship, told them, as often as they did it, to remember him. **[Quiet Moments with God Devotional; Sunset with God, 6th Edition, Pg. 135.]**

Just as the bread and wine offered by Melchizedek was meant to refresh and rejuvenate Abraham's physical strength, the bread and wine that we partake of at the Lord's Table has the same effect on our spiritual life and strength. That is why the Apostle Paul cautions us that if we partake of the bread and wine at the Lord's Table in an unworthy manner, it will result in spiritual weakness in our bodies.

1 Corinthians 11:29-30 *29 "For he that eateth and drinketh unworthily, eateth and drinketh damnation to himself, not discerning the Lord's body.*

> 30 For this cause many are weak and sickly among you, and many sleep."

Bread and wine were suitable refreshment for people who are faint and weary. In this case, for Abraham and the members of his household who went out to battle. In the case of David and his followers it was when he was ministered to by Barzillai the Gileadite in Mahanaim during his troublesome escape from his dear Son Absalom who pursued him to overthrow him and take his Kingdom.

II Samuel 17:27-29

> 27 "And it came to pass, when David was come to Mahanaim, that Shobi the son of Nahash of Rabbah of the children of Ammon, and Machir the son of Ammiel of Lodebar, and Barzillai the Gileadite of Rogelim,
>
> 28 Brought beds, and basons, and earthen vessels, and wheat, and barley, and flour, and parched corn, and beans, and lentiles, and parched pulse,

29 And honey, and butter, and sheep, and cheese of kine, for David, and for the people that were with him, to eat: for they said, The people is hungry, and weary, and thirsty, in the wilderness."

But wait and see the agony that David and his men endured before they were miraculously ministered to by Barzillai the Gileadite and the other well-wishers. Before this, Ziba had lied unto David about Mephibosheth, Absalom had slept with his father David's concubines on the roof top, Ahitophel had betrayed the trust of David as David's counselor and Shimei, a relative of King Saul had bitterly cursed out David.

II Samuel 16: 5-8

5 "And when king David came to Bahurim, behold, thence came out a man of the family of the house of Saul, whose name was Shimei, the son of Gera: he came forth, and cursed still as he came.

6 And he cast stones at David, and at all the servants of king David: and all the people and all the mighty men were on his right hand and on his left.

7 And thus said Shimei when he cursed, Come out, come out, thou bloody man, and thou man of Belial:

8 The Lord hath returned upon thee all the blood of the house of Saul, in whose stead thou hast reigned; and the Lord hath delivered the kingdom into the hand of Absalom thy son: and, behold, thou art taken in thy mischief, because thou art a bloody man."

How much more was left to come upon David until he and the hungry men who were with him were miraculously ministered unto by Barzillai and company? It is remarkable that Christ appointed the same bread and wine as the memorials of his body and blood, which are meat and drink indeed to the soul.

Note a very interesting similarity between the Office of Melchizedek and that of Our Lord Jesus

"Melchizedek blessed Abram from God (through the bread and wine he ministered to Abraham). And Melchizedek Blessed God from Abram (through the tithes Abraham paid to him). So in effect Melchizedek is serving in the role of a mediator between God and man.

And so is Our Lord Jesus; who in his person came as the mediator between God and man. As a confirmation to Jesus' role as a mediator, **I Timothy 2:5** assert that; *"For there is one God, and one mediator between God and Men, the man Christ Jesus"* as also he said in another place *"I am the way, the truth and the life; no man cometh unto the Father but by me."*

"Melchizedek was a mediator between God and man; representing God by holding out the hand of mercy, and representing man by reaching forth the hand of faith" [Barne's Notes]

The blessing bestowed upon Abraham by Melchizedek was a part of the priest's office. He was to bless in the name of the Lord, forever and to wish and pray for a blessing on others as dictated to the priest of old by God; *"23) Speak unto Aaron and unto his sons, saying, On this wise ye shall bless the children of Israel, saying unto them 24) The Lord bless thee, and keep thee; 25) The Lord make his face shine upon thee; and be gracious unto thee 26) The LORD lift up his countenance upon thee, and give thee peace."* **Numbers 6:23-26.**

Just as Abraham was blessed; there fell upon him a great darkness.

It is worth noting that in the proceeding Chapter (Genesis 15) after Abraham had met Melchizedek then it was revealed to him about the great darkness that was to afflict his descendants and posterity.

Genesis 15:12-13 *"12) Now when the sun was going down, a deep sleep fell upon Abram; and behold, terror and great darkness fell upon him. 13) And he said unto Abram, Know of a surety that thy seed shall be a stranger in a land that is not theirs, and shall serve them; and they shall afflict them four hundred years."*

Is that not the same thing that happened to the disciples after Jesus had comforted them and blessed them with all blessings and great promises had been given unto them; they then entered into great persecution in Jerusalem.

It is no secret that at times, it is after some of our greatest accomplishments and divine encounters with the Lord that we fall under the spell of great discouragement and depression. This is no different from what happened to Elijah the great prophet of God. It was after he had called down fire from heaven to consume his sacrifice in order to prove to the prophets of Baal, the might and power of the Almighty God, that he started to complain to God and to run away from the threats of Jezebel the princess of Baal.

So, what is the purpose of drawing these similarities between Christ and Melchizedek?

Abraham in paying tithes to Melchizedek, is acknowledging the inferiority of his great grandson's priesthood through Levi and the tribe of Levi. The book of Hebrew tells us that... *"Levi also, who receiveth tithes, payed tithes in Abraham."*

For he was yet in the loins of his father, when Melchisedec met him.

If † therefore perfection were by the Levitical priesthood, † (for under it the people received the law,) what further need was there that another priest should rise after the order of Melchisedec, and not be called after the order of Aaron? **Hebrews 7: 9-14.**

In other words Abraham was not only acknowledging his inferiority to Melchizedek but at the same time, he was also acknowledging the inferiority of the order of the Levitical priesthood to the order of Melchizedek's priesthood. This is indeed a profound revelation in that although Levi was not yet born, Levi's order of priesthood over Israel had already been subjected to the order of priesthood of Melchizedek hundreds of years prior to the birth of Levi who is one of the great grandsons of Abraham through Isaac first and then Jacob. This is just like God, for he knows the end of a thing even before its' beginning.

Levi paying tithes through the loins of Abraham, hundreds of years before he was born, goes to show us that we inherit souls from our human parent. This is contrary to the belief of many that there exist in heaven some sort of a pool of souls from which souls are dispatched into humans at birth.

Notice that the new covenant is not founded upon Law of Moses nor on the Levitical priesthood but rather upon the power of an endless life, which is a gift of God through His Son Jesus Christ. This is because the believer in Jesus Christ is born of God, and of God's Holy Spirit and according to the bible, God dwells within the believer. That is why no one could claim they were born of God until Christ came.

To be under the old covenant you have to obey the laws of Moses; but to be under the new covenant you don't necessarily have to obey the commandments of Paul. However it will be very unwise if one can't see that the instructions given by Paul in the Epistles is God speaking to us even under the instructions of Paul. For example, when Paul admonished women not to have short hair, can't you see that it makes them look even better and differentiates women from people of the opposite gender? Will you blatantly ignore it and not obey it because you are not under the law? That will certainly be unwise.

Finally, the power of an endless life creates Sons under the new covenant instead of Servants under the old covenant. Hebrew 7:19 says the law made nothing perfect; but Christ did which results in perfect salvation.

According to Hebrew 8:7 the second covenant was made because the first one was faulty. So the new covenant is perfect because it does what the old cannot do, in that it gives you a new heart. God is done with the old covenant and he is not going to resurrect it anymore.

God has abolished the old covenant for good. It is finished he said on the cross and never to be resurrected. As a result, Hebrew 4:16 therefore commends us to come boldly unto to the throne of grace that we may obtain mercy, and find grace to help in time of need.

How many of you are scared of the Lord Jesus and of his presence in His church. The book of Hebrew said he is holy but harmless, meaning you can touch him and die because he is holy but you can also touch him and live forever because He is harmless.

Your love for the Lord and your knowledge of him should not scare you away from him. It should rather draw you more and more towards him. The reason why many draw away from Him is because they have not gotten to really know the Lord. They only know about the Lord, which entirely different from knowing Him.

It is worth noting that the usage of the verb 'to know' in the Hebrew language is not as shallow as we find it in the English language. To know' is the word *'Ginosko' in the* Greek which means 'absolute knowledge.' That is knowing with all surety.

Furthermore in the Hebrew, the word 'intercourse' is used to express ones' true knowledge of a thing, subject or person. This is because "to know"; is used as the Jewish idiomatic expressions for sexual intercourse between a man and a woman. This explains why many times in the Old Testament one comes across phrases like; "and Adam knew his wife and she bore him a son" or Jacob knew his wife and the ultimate results was the birth of a baby. This usage of obviously far deeper than the way it's expressed in the English language.

And that's why we should be very careful that; some day when we stand before the Lord; that he doesn't say to us; "Depart from me ye workers of iniquity for I know ye not

---

Today, we have a generation that knows a whole lot about God; but who don't know God, and that is a spiritual tragedy.

Knowing about God therefore is not to know about Him from the bible but rather as the bible declares; "no man knoweth the father but the son and to whom the son may reveal him."

Knowing God comes as a result of direct, and miraculous revelation of God, and once you get it, no man can take it away from you. If you haven't received it, no matter what you do you really don't have it; that is until you receive it God's way through His prescribed new birth experience.

Your faith should not rest in the scripture- it ought to rest entirely in God, to the extent that even when the scriptures is taken away from you; you would still be a Christian.

Some Christians may seize to be Christians when they lose their bible, but for you, who are born of his Spirit and washed in his blood; even when you lose the holy scriptures you can still declare; "thy word have I hidden in my heart that I may not sin against you." Simply because the logos which is Christ himself and which is the true word live inside of you. Isn't that beautiful? This is important because as you grow older, chances are, you may lose your memory as part of the process of growing old, but even if you lose your memory, you will not lose your beloved because he dwells inside of you.

The Act of Worship

This 3 series tape will leave you amused and enlightened but definitely not bored. It is an in depth exposition of Psalm 149 and reveals how true worship should be in the sanctuary of our God based on the meaning of the common word Hallelujah. (Halal Yah)

The Wise but Unfaithful Steward

God has always entrusted his work on earth into the hands of men. While some have been found to be faithful, others have not. This 2 series message brings out a clear distinction between faithful and unfaithful servants of the Lord.

The Ministry of Jesus and John

This intriguing message will leave you well enlightened about the ministries of Jesus and John. Symbolically speaking each of them had a 3 days in which to fulfill their ministry on earth. See how these three days plays out in the life and ministry of each character.

Why Elijah Must Go, and Elisha Must Come

Did you know that Elijah's ministry represented the old covenant and Elisha's the new covenant? This tape brings out clearly how this is possible through the various miracles that each men performed. While Elijah began his ministry by calling down fire which is a type of judgement, Elisha on the other hand started his ministry with a blessing of the healing of the waters of Samaria.

Ephraim; Fruitful in Affliction

As we know, Joseph had two sons namely Ephraim and Manasseh. Ephraim, although the younger of the two, had the blessing of the first born bestowed upon him. The meaning is his name is; Fruitful in the land of affliction. Find out how his name played out in his destiny and posterity.

The Spirit of the Lion and the Lamb

This message is a timely message for those who have exhausted their strength in the Lord as lion and are wondering what next is there for them to conquer and how to conquer. John in the book of Revelation was told to behold a lion and when he turned to see, he beheld a lamb instead. What does this mean?

The Iinterlude to the Conquest of Canaan

Have you ever read about a Canaanite tribe in the bible by name the Gibeonites? Find out how God used this little tribe to deceive Joshua and Israel and also how by their deception, Gentles were engrafted into the salvation plan of God. A very unusual but interesting story that will leave you educated in God's plan of salvation.

The Story of Noah; Tracing the Origin of the Black Race

Growing up as a little child in Africa, I was told in my Sunday school class that the black race has experienced much poverty and misery because the progenitor of the race is Ham who was cursed by Noah. As an adult, I studied my bible only to discover that Ham was not cursed but rather it was Canaan who was cursed.

The Connection between Moral, Spiritual and Physical Laws

Is there any connection between the moral, physical and spiritual laws of nature? Yes, there certainly is. Find out from this tape how the three laws are inter-connected one to the other.

Limiting the Holy One of Israel

Do you still believe that God can do all things? Well, good for you because there are others who don't believe this anymore. Isn't that sad. This tape deals with how Israel limited the power of God and paid a dare price for their unbelief.

Vineyard Parables

Our Lord Jesus told a set of parables that are commonly called the vineyard parables. Each of these parables brings out the clear distinction between Kingdom-sons and Kingdom-servants. Are all sons as some believe? Or there are Sons and there are servants in God's Kingdom. Find out from this tape what differentiates a Kingdom-son from a servant.

The Three Seed Parable

The 3 seed parables as told by Jesus, and like any other parable has a specific lesson for us to learn and apply to our lives.

This two-part series will leave you enlightened and surely educated in the word of God.

Why Revival Tarries

As end-time believers in the Lord Jesus, we all desire to have great revival. Many people have many reasons why true revival tarries. This tape answers that question in a way that will leave you thinking but will also leave you yarning to prepare yourself for a great end-time move of God's Spirit.

The Application of the Blood

This tape deals with the legacy that Christ left for his beloved church and bride as a result of his death, burial and resurrection. Find out what this legacy is and how you can tap into it for your spiritual victory.

The Act of Sin & the State of Sin

The act of sin has always been confused with the state of sin. Are the tow the same thing or there is indeed a difference. Find out from this tape what the state of sin is and how different it is from the act of sin.

The Sleeping Church

One of the greatest signs of the end time will be spiritual slumber and sleeping. Are you part of a sleeping church or a church that is militant? It is for you to decide what church you belong to.

Waiting upon the Lord

Most people in church today knows the scriptural reference that says "they that wait upon the Lord shall renew their strength." But only a few really knows how to wait upon the Lord. Find out from this message on how to really wait on the Lord.

The Law of the First Fruit

This tape deals with the principle behind 'First Fruits'. Do you know that this principle embodies everything from the beginning till the coming of our Lord Jesus? Even during his coming, he will first and foremost reap the first fruit of souls who died in him before he reaps the general harvest of souls. Sounds complicated but this message makes it clear and very simple.

The Principle of Tithing & Offering

This tape deals with the legacy that Christ Jesus handed over to his new testament church and to very believer who is willing to exercise this authority in his name.

The Prodigal Father

Contrary to the parable of our Lord Jesus that has become known as 'the prodigal Son'; This tape reveals the heavenly father us being 'prodigal' and not the son.

Your understanding of this 3 Part series message depends on how you define the word 'prodigal'. This word has nothing to do with one who run away from home. It has to do with one who gives away of his own goods freely and lavishly. That therefore defines the fathers love and care towards his Son than it describes the son's actions which are more rebellious than being prodigal.

Abba - Father

One of the greatest privilege God bestowed upon humanity is to allow us to address Him as our Father.

As simple as it may be, it makes all the difference for the new testament church. The great prophets, priest and patriarchs of old never had that privilege. Not even the angelic host in heaven had that privilege.

Divine Empowerment

This tape deals with the legacy that Christ Jesus handed over to his new testament church and to very believer who is willing to exercise this authority in his name.

Circle of Friends - Chose Wisely, Chose Godly

Your friends define part of who you really are. There are levels of friendship and associations. Even Jesus choose the 72 and out of that, later chose the 12 disciple. And thereafter he chose the 3 (Peter, James and John) who would become his inner circle throughout his earthly ministry. You chose your friends, don't let them chose you.

Love So Amazing

Do you know that the most popular verse in the bible' John 3:16 was part of a conversation that our Lord Jesus had with Nicodemus?

The love of God reaches farther than our minds can comprehend. God is supreme but also a loving father. He is all powerful but also a caring father.

The Order of Melchizedek

This tape deals with the being and person of Melchizedek who is recognized as the most mysterious and unaccountable of all historical bible characters. In what ways was his order of priesthood different from the Levitical priesthood but similar to that of our Lord Jesus. This tape' approach to this topic will leave you amused, instructed, enlightened, stirred up, and challenged, but definitely not bored.

The Breaking & Making of a True Disciple

Have you ever heard the words of that popular; Break me, melt me and Mold me? That is what our Lord Jesus did with his disciple Peter. A painful process as it may be for us, the persecution and trial of our faith makes us strong. Every believer at some point in time would go through the breaking, melting and molding of their faith, so Get Ready.

The Kingdom Series

This is an 8 series tape that talks about adopting a kingdom mentality in our service to advance God's Kingdom on earth. Don't be caught up in your own little world of ministry. The Kingdom of God is far greater than our little local churches. Reach out when the opportunity comes, to minister unto others who are outside of your church. You have nothing to lose but all to gain when you adopt a Kingdom mentality.

Maranatha - The Lord Cometh

This tape is deals with the desire about the coming of the Lord that is somehow uncommon in today's church.

Maranatha meaning; Lord Come Quick, use to be the greetings of the early saints of the New Testament church. Today, we hardly hear preaching about the coming of the Lord in our churches.

Made in the USA
Middletown, DE
02 March 2019